MW00906787

BENEATH
THE GLASS BELL

POEMS
ALEC EKMEKJI

Printed by CreateSpace, 2018, an Amazon.Com Company
ISBN: 978-1726083430

Contents

"A writer should have the precision of a poet and the imagination of a scientist."

V. Nabokov

The Primordial Soup
(A Prologue)

pushing field monosyllabic lla leisure curvature squares hid thumb inspire
suspend doll punctuated sequel rhythms saving peaks shirts left lit dauhgter
made both goodnight hues bench at sea who silence your reinserts mother
whose colorful do cooled sun surprised dreams panic-stricken floors come
he gone shoves home be flayed flakes foot balls slivers pastoral palms Dirac
spaces wolgnoom domes woven sentences boyish beneath fading bell Baudelaire
showing watch laugh planted cups wool fashionable clean know blooming
queen Arioso friends spine man viewing hears dying wonder alcoholic lullabies
water unlike windy diaries only presses western married knows seems clash Ri-
ngo novel behind sobbed Ninochka Will chords imagined edge tiny except
diverging love gashed Van oblivious deck parallel moonlight sailors wept en-
tangled Perforate Cool than unborn tied slacks tremble rising Paul drippings
toward drip island dispassionate hot youth knew increments flowerbeds wrin-
kle og stranded Somehow wing gather travel two lurk grown strings bride
promised boxes wall fool near awe thrashes gentle seeping ask sees sit sleeps
quartet scoops selects proposes ceiling graveled diffuse John moon father run
shared   seduction With evening then collect nose song windmills my peach
blouse festive poked shriek suit Mrs. Build natives off noisy now pores tempest
mind ripe Gagarin Lara read unveiled roads falling all bridge nannies backlit
bow raging a springtime plum gray Shepard bone mango older stained mak-
ing time tear remember bed lithe adult so passion Rogers Russian tsum stain
some brothers mouth toils recesses Sonia waiting does tired tomorrow Stan-
wyck shattered giggle sun if doorwindow availed emergency pile unfamiliar
dispiteous collected whites without Rolls arrays Jung Ear over Teddy marry
chamber fresh city cold bleak minds whispering yesterday where glows spleen
phosphorous creep shall not its to Cervantes half-torn late scintillating carry
their prisms Starr giggled tfel long Loving hall twins earth greeted slice among
lanterns warm watching homeward down searched sleeping we folds palace
sweet rise small veiled wearied Stories cursing tales waves bones photograph
balloon village febrile bought smell homes had bathtub wind Dulcinea disperse
upon boy is horse poet words accompanied girl who Carlos don't shadows you
sign wood disparate balances glides glass give knot writhe breath must of el-
evator sail next breakfast sky put floe crawls far them magician nights fur-
tive restful young float in tin was checkout buckled hospital it Margot lie up
spring husbands rhyme heralding palm swam around can moist fine sought
she busy jagged whips slight edged rays about woman tables bathing trian-
gulates years echoes page cheerfully taut tender closes standing sheets de-
vouring laughed someone gold enough revel flint though are distance tucking

blend Murano veil shedding rubble lips little carried silhouettes wore museum figure Jim knees right winter thgir the glide bread open hand rosewood shed other pass plums gnisahc belongings want sunny thongs Wayne comb dance throat whispered God choruses die laurels nurse buttoned ignition wetted invents caps San Juan Hill stom I wrinkled loose into devour setacoffus pleasures seamless book tonight bear turn variations grass soften gifts Pavlova on always charmed loud delight discovered raft you're felled save big wakes adorn washed sitting return him trucks raspberry lovers become clings faces speak intricately side and clay herself apple Don Quixote leads branches forehead paying cutting afternoon silk scissors walked found nighttime weep silken reds daylight went panes watchman shudder heart graves tell discolored street ancient gasp ni wife permitted vertigo each morning guess mercifully seem pressed guides wasteful daze face snowflakes fashioned beyond fractured what's merging slid smooth stairs Dame reads dozen many any her freshly seconds wolf more soft intruders area hells arm wailing Astaire once melting whistling squished ten ivory raking canon signed fall holding fingers past beverages ramp lover seen hope silvered they mast twice wobnair which latches Debussy maple how briefcase pruner Quasimodo polysyllabic hearts moving born gathers blow reticent sounds riverbank step new men or grace suddenly lay roses puddle mine else dreaming blade stroll even cultivated guiding darling Raskolnikov Hemmingway wives Hollywood carved fountains there pen dare written balding tones died soon pebble footsteps this cleanse future one slide glaze as day lovingly sister urns violin stood before moonless our growls also held soaked twinkle tongue-lashing slow Grushenka were caption thumbs place bubbles babies resonating frozen blue cream walk luminous bare broken finding adventure Glenn coming reshapes line iron engines nword uoy tamed shop dispenses string hurry blackened row sullied thought choosing swallow feet blood fling belly reading clothes head chiseled desperate sparks toys says yet pizzicato climb hcaer celluloid create handed shows tears son would flesh beauty could doorless lure windows another bid cloudless sand am viola exile donned it's sadness fills wanted vibrating constructed glass-blower enliven gave bedtime Cagney graceful away angels cliff rains reach sun-drenched fell pool munching keep admiring restless fled icebergs gardener downtown fragments breastsprobing fellow cobble-stoned built take shadow sewed shoes fair flames from large when gliding appears ice strides lifeguard too blink pressing walls America tombstone across softly work gone label between sober perhaps leaves arrives eht Roy lighthouses these thirst for wouldn't cautions minutes discarding path hellish knowing rose Rossiniana autumn Beethoven wearing hurled carpenter Elizabeth floating lanes dinner been brought Roosevelt searching lots swerving protruding gently cracks emulsion sons glasses bled air hold gathering mist shoe lungs abandoned yes keys bag duty crumpled gracefully fruit but prepares done heads suns bumper rehearsing glances led snoom hides plump tells coated sleep purple dark apprentice

lies steps coils bold double eight like same have explain petals strain light
heaven skin easily heavenly reel dolphins hear burst divide pebbles quark
delicate family becoming memory consoles enter traffic barber tilting know-
ingly sing knives butterflies wide ot craters well leave touch forgiven sea cello
anew translucent parking dear wish skating coffins poise oak stars summer
joy hair easy cannot way rides anhiding dripped resist rules veil might make
wild Verlaine us whispers playing Panama fondled marble Technicolor hope-
lessness rigid tips signals laughing weightless sawed clears planned mag-
ic shrouded let's chime pulse names frames bottom stones lull parents bath
by suits tongue brush said wooden transparent horizon that rake entered at
Cliburn hushed nor sold sunken dew lane hand under Virgil slept old re-
vealing heavens own conform stranger twinkled white drink plastic days
sate appetites voices Apassionata instants peeled falls syllables Bishop Ravel
eventually hourglasses garden hitting boisterous slats grand swims eyes rav-
ages sidewalk midair took ships breathless dead approached slowly skeleton
black out Magritte park cast quietly glass stop possibilities silent vanilla nails
sometimes try terrified secret me rumble caverns retrieves windowless six-
teen continue after pulled midnight pull along car-pool sunlight night snow
invite floor no brake dancing say hush begged sank back gaze hat hell grass
inside surprise green buttons lost red although thinner meet winter first has
reassembles smile entombed pear women apart balcony get moonglow letter
tempers hours quickly oh throehtlahelpleh trade see jump just through charge
thrash almost plans things going begin white parts tall room adrift stings
shimmering golf thunder tongue edge shall solitude si together picture sent
faceless wine cuffs nudes whether gate children told savored flash thin ladies
smeared soared five single converging eyelids changed ashore look scattered
mirror shoulders lavish borne roam stand onto wait reached forks unveiled
kiss imperceptible stars above neither here caged part meter his why noises
hands silver bifocal front Faulkner such soles supermarket sorrow against
wanting lick dunes wake everything sat sharp clasps weight cats pieces car

. . . .

Beauty

I want you to read this
As I write it
Because I like you,
Because you're like me.

No, not impatient,
I want you to read this
As I write it,
Commit it to memory
As I end it.

Beauty is in the remembering.
The present is a tasteless trick.
Look! here comes the rabbit, Magician!
It is uncovering its face,
As usual.

Do you remember
The texture of its mask?

Just Like That

Just like that
He found a girl,
He found a riverbank,

Just like that
She lay her back
On the knowing grass,

Just like that
He found her lips,
He found her buttoned blouse,

Just like that
He married,
He married someone else.

Now sometimes she sees him
At the riverbank,
Looking for loose gold buttons
In the dew on the grass.

On Ravel's String Quartet

There is a place under your skin
Where hides a pizzicato violin.

In your belly swims a cello;
I pull your hair and make a bow.

Inside your throat a viola crawls,
The bow thrashes on palace walls.

White fingers wait behind taut lips;
They smell of freshly wetted whips.

The viola coils, the cello stings,
And I am entangled in the strings
Of your pizzicato violin.

To the Sea

"Butterflies fall to the sea..." Czeslaw Milosz

Give me a bath tonight my darling,
Not a tongue-lashing
But a bath of warm water and bubbles,
Monosyllabic and polysyllabic bubbles
That rise from the sea like dolphins
And suspend over their wake for long instants,
And suspend in the mist of their wake for long instants
Before falling into the sea as butterflies,
Monosyllabic and polysyllabic butterflies
That take away with them my breath to the sea,
My breathless gasps that hurry to the sea
To soften the fall of your butterflies,
Your butterflies over the dark devouring sea,
They hurry to the sea.

Becoming Paul Dirac

$$\int_{-\infty}^{+\infty} \delta(x)dx = 1$$

Even the woman -
Even the woman
Standing in wool slacks
That strain at the cuffs
Reading a letter
While munching a plum
Will not be surprised
At how gracefully
Drippings from her mouth
Stain the written words
Before seeping through
To the other side of
Of the page in her hand.

Lament

And yet the sky
Dispenses with her gifts,
Somehow,
And out of her blue
Winter shoves summer away.
Branches shudder,
And the wind shows the leaves the way
To there where lie restful,
Wasteful,
Imagined plans
To sail long ships to the sun.

Beneath the Glass Bell

And to hear silence
She closes all her eyes,
She lies on bare grass
Beneath a glass bell
In a field hushed by
Winter's frozen light.
But a song gathers
At the tips of her eyes
To rhythms of dew
Blooming into ice,
And on the sun's rays
In her bell of glass
She hears the tempest
Gathering in the lungs
Of the glass-blower
Sleeping in Murano.

Cervantes Invents the Novel

Eventually
we lost interest.

I brought home a dozen boxes
to divide our belongings.
When everything was collected,
except the books,
we sat on the floor
across each other
and searched through them
one by one.

She wanted the Faulkners
I wanted the Hemingways
she put her hands on the Jungs
- I told her she could have them -
she handed me the Baudelaire
- told me it was only fair -
and I gave her Don Quixote
to hear her Dulcinea laugh
one last time.

When she went to turn off the lights
I took her notebook of diaries
and hid it beneath my pile,
saving it for a windy night
when I would tear off its pages
and fling them at the windmills
to watch them float one by one
to the dark side
of the sky.

Old Man Carlos

The old man
(Balding)
In the white suit
(Wrinkled)
Standing in front of me
In the supermarket
Checkout line
Paying for plums
(Plastic bag)
That will drip on his suit
At breakfast
Does not know that
I am watching him,
Admiring his delicate,
Almost boyish hands,
Just as I don't know
Which plum in my bag it was
That he had fondled
Before discarding it
And choosing another,
More ripe,
More plump,
More purple.

Charmed Quark

for Murray Gell-Mann

There is a dark figure in the distance
That could be you,
But across a bridge all cats look gray
And I will wish you are she.
Your magic is showing
Through the glass veil of possibilities.
Will you turn gently as I fall through the veil?
Will you walk softly as I fall at your feet?
No one dare hold such beauty for long.
Walk quickly when I fall.

Arioso

How do you explain
To the tired nurse
In the hospital's
Emergency room
That you gashed your head
When you told your boy
That your love for him
Fills you like a balloon,
That you will burst soon,
And he giggled and laughed,
And he held your head with his little hands,
And he poked your eyes with his soft fingers,
And he squished your nose with his tiny thumb,
And he pulled your lips, tied them in a knot,
And sent you floating toward the ceiling?

Variations on Magritte

Say that you are here.
Say that you are *here*. Say
I am here.

Say I am here
Like the sun-drenched rains
Of some summer days
Restless I am here,

Say I am here
Like the peeled moon
Of some cloudless nights,
Faceless I am here,

Say I am here
Like the rose entombed
In the painting of the rose,
Weightless I am here,

Say I am here
Like the magician's apple,
Hurled from the canon's mouth
Breathless I am here.

A Hollywood Sequel

Sometimes
In some warm summer nights of autumn
When the sun triangulates its gaze
On the day shedding its skin,
Revealing....

Sometimes
When the nightwatchman latches the museum gates,
And the five nudes holding hands
Begin their pastoral dance, as if
Rehearsing...

Sometimes
When the blade glides into moist skin
And the skin falls between folds of sullied sheets
Revealing the flesh of a sweet peach,
Or a pear...

Sometimes
When fountains thirst in cobble-stoned city squares
And the shadows of footsteps
Walk past the puddle next to the bed,
Quietly...

Then,
Sometimes then,
When all appears as it is not
As Sonia sleeps among rolls of celluloid sheets,
When all seems as it must have been,
Raskolnikov wakes.

Moonglow

Cool
The moon I know
Knowingly glows
Beneath my bare soles
As I step gently,
Gently step,
Try to step gently
Among craters.

But ancient pebbles
Perforate the skin
And create craters anew
That creep into the souls
Of me and the moon and I wonder:
Why be a
Fool?

Adventure

She sought adventure.
So she sawed her bed and built a raft,
So she sold her lover and bought a mast,
So she sewed his shirts and fashioned a sail
And soared to the sea.

She reached the island of dunes and sand,
So she sawed her lover and cast him adrift,
So she soaked her sail - he sobbed in the sea -
So she sank her raft and swam ashore
To conform her spine to the dunes of sand.

But she had stranded herself on an island
Where the natives greeted her
In their leisure suits
In their Panama hats
In their colorful thongs
In their ice cream trucks.

Oh how she begged to lick double scoops
Of passion fruit, wild raspberry,
Mango, mango...
But it was vanilla
That cooled the pores
Of her melting tongue.

The Ravages of Snowflakes

The snow fell in small increments around us
And not even the flash of youth
Could save us from the ravages of its flakes;
Who knows how to build lighthouses on raging waves?

We entered the grand caverns without lanterns,
On our shoulders we carried urns made of clay,
We lit our way with the sparks of sharp flintstones
With which we signed our names on the palace walls,
And the walls bled into our urns as petals
Which we scattered on our foreheads like laurels
As the snow fell in small increments around us.

We now gather in abandoned open fields,
We sit around tables constructed of wood,
We drink our wine from discolored tin cups
On whose stained walls roam the flames that led our way,
And to keep warm we bear our children in our minds
As the snow falls in small increments around us.

On Viewing a Photograph of Elizabeth Bishop

Is she sitting or standing?
I cannot tell she does not tell her secret...
Does my gaze brush her eyelids?
I cannot tell she will not tell her secret...
Will my backlit gasp reach her ears?
I cannot tell how can she tell her secret?

The emulsion that once savored
The black and white phosphorus kiss of her lips
Now scarcely clings to the blackened white skin and hair,
Clings with a might now bleak, now slight,
With a sadness cultivated in solitude.

She was a sober poet it said
Now dead
In the caption at the bottom of the page.
I would ask me to marry her
But it's too late: I am not dead.

To Russian Ladies Wanting to Marry

What's become of you Grushenka,
Where have your Gagarins gone?
Your eyes gaze on America
To be bride to Jim or John?

Virgil is long dead Grushenka,
Shepard is hitting golf balls,
John Glenn kisses babies now,
And when Astaire kisses Ninotchka
She glows in reds and whites, blue.

Roy Roger's horse died Grushenka,
John Wayne rides the western sky,
Cagney growls at the angels now
And Lara has abandoned hope
Of finding you, Grushenka.

Whose heart you want Grushenka?
Ringo Starr is a barber now,
Van Cliburn's hands are ivory now,
And when Dame Margot dances,
She dances caged in glass now.

What's become of you Grushenka?
Pavlova wouldn't know you now.
Where have our Gagarins gone?

Air's Gentle Wrinkle

In my morning days one night
I discovered that
The horizon's stars twinkle,
And on many summer nights
I twinkled with the stars.
Then one day suddenly
Someone older than me
Told me stars don't twinkle,
That it's the air's gentle wrinkle
That makes stars seem to blink.
All this said and done,
My morning days gone,
Your forehead has become
My horizon's skies…
I sing you lullabies,
I blow air in your eyes,
I twinkle with my stars.

Parallel Roads

We travel on parallel roads you and I,
We come upon desperate forks, you and I,
But the sun's rays grace both our steps,
You and I,
Mine in awe of the shadow
Whispering laughing behind me,
You oblivious of the shadow
Guiding your way lovingly.

Yes, we travel parallel roads you and I;
It is written that we shall part you and I
When we reach our disparate forks,
You and I,
Yours diverging into lavish
Choruses of colorful dreams,
Like the sun's rays resonating
In arrays of shimmering prisms,
Mine converging mercifully
With the echoes of once-dreamt hues
Homeward, homeward to that tender
Seamless white of the restful moon.

Exile and Seduction

First they take away father.
They return the same evening
And take away his belongings:
His clothes, his shoes,
His stories and songs.
Mother does not know how to resist the intruders
And consoles us with fractured sentences,
With words shattered into jagged-edged syllables
Like the family photographs
Hurled onto the grand mirror in the hall.

The tall man wearing an unfamiliar hat
Parts the lull of the next afternoon
With measured strides.
"I am your new father", he says,
And as mother prepares dinner
He leads us into the hall
And guides us down onto our hands and our knees
Among the fragments of wood and glass.

I collect the broken frames
And place the pieces in father's hands,
Sister clears the shattered glass
And retrieves the photographs,
Father reassembles the wooden frames
By pushing in the protruding nails with his thumbs
And reinserts the pictures,
Tucking their edges beneath the lips of the ancient wood,
Then from the rubble of yesterday
He selects the large pieces of silvered glass
And reshapes them with his long and graceful tongue,
And presses them over the pictures, into the frames,
And into the recesses of our minds.

Pool Rules

No lifeguard on duty here.
Children under sixteen
Must be accompanied by an adult.
No alcoholic beverages.
No glass permitted in pool area.
No loud noises after eight p.m.
Pool closes at ten p.m.
Give me a bathtub any day
And you, my love.

The Mirror

The apprentice to the royal carpenter
Proposes to built a hiding place
Behind the mirror
In the chamber of the queen,
Wide enough for two.

Let's build it young fellow!

But the old man cautions that
Such things can be seen only
When the skin is flayed and peeled in slivers,
When the bone is carved and the blood washed clean,
When the flesh is sliced and smeared on smooth glass,
Thin,
Translucent,
And pressed even thinner, almost transparent,
By the weight of the falling silvered skin.

In the Garden of Dreams

In the garden
Where neither hope nor hopelessness
Pulse along,

The gardener toils
Moving from tombstone to tombstone
Cheerfully,

Cutting the grass
Around the protruding marble heads
Held rigid,

Raking dead leaves
That continue to fall on men,
Even in sleep,

Always dreaming
Of that fine day just beyond the
Horizon,

When he will trade
His rake for comb and his pruner
For scissors

And open shop
On a busy noisy boisterous
Downtown street.

Gather Around

Gather around
All little boys
Gather around,
It is nighttime
Although bedtime
Gather around,
Morning arrives,
Thunder arrives,
It is springtime
Autumn arrives,
Thunder arrives,
To the clash of
Voices, echoes,
Thunder arrives.

On Beethoven's Apassionata

When I enter heaven - and I will enter heaven -
It will be a heaven of my own making,
Unlike the heavens of fashionable men,
A heaven where the days sail to the minutes
And where the seconds glide into the years,
Where hourglasses, coated with hellish glaze,
Revel in the dance of the years minutes days.

And when I enter hell - yes, I will enter hell -
It will be a hell fashioned by my hands,
Unlike the hells of dispassionate men,
A hell where the hours swallow the days,
And where the minutes devour the years,
Where the heavenly sands, falling, in a daze,
Suspend in midair to kiss that hellish glaze.

Debussy Waiting Under Verlaine's Balcony

But how to tell the lights and sounds
Of night apart easily

When the moon tells the sun's bold tales
In whispered tones

And the glass panes on the windows
Of village homes

Diffuse these tales by vibrating
In silver chords

And disperse them in the spaces
On marble floors

Scintillating to the whispers
Of young girls' soles?

veiled women

veiled women veiled in silk and black,
women veiled furtive in dark,
lurk beneath windowless doors
of shrouded doorless domes.

veiled women lie in dying light...

veiled women veiled in silent green,
women veiled bathing in spleen,
weep for sons who will not weep,
hush daughters, bid them to sleep.

veiled we men poise by moonlight...

veiled women un-veiled in moonlight,
women veiled lunimous white,
reel beneath the silhouettes
of dispiteous appetites.

veiled women tear at midnight...

veiled women veiled reticent red,
women veiled availed unveiled,
slice fresh bread with wooden knives
cleanse false leaves between men's eyes

veiled women die at sunlight...

veiled women veiled in wailing white,
women veiled to earth's delight,
lure false coffins with their writhe
shriek in coffins silken, white...

veiled women wait for daylight...

Your Bones

No one could tell this
by watching you from that distance
as you waited on the bench
on the cliff above the sea.

I had promised to meet you there
but I was late.
Was I too late?
From that distance I could not tell
whether you thought I was late
as I walked toward the wooden bench
where you were sitting
watching the sun thrash on the waves.
I wanted to surprise you
even though I knew
I was late
and I walked along the sidewalk's edge
so you would not see me
coming to meet you
from the far side of the waves.

But when I stood behind you,
when I slid my hands over your eyes
to ask you to guess who,
your face crumpled in my palms,
your back buckled on the wooden slats,
your fingers dripped through the cracks.

Yet I was surprised
when I approached you
at how little you had changed
over the years...
except your bones...
your bones
that had grown tired
of waiting for me.

Going Home (a waltz)

Going home is so easy...
A goodnight,
A briefcase,
Elevator.

Going home can be easy...
The car keys,
Parking brake,
Ignition.

Going home is sometimes easy...
A stop sign,
A red light,
A green light.

Going home appears so easy...
The on-ramp,
The car-pool lane,
Merging.

Going home only appears easy...
Cars swerving,
No signals,
No brake lights.

Going home is not so easy...
Cutting lanes,
Cursing flames,
Bumper sounds.

Going home, I tell you, is not easy...
Traffic cold,
Engines hot,
Tempers wild.

Going home was once so easy...
Lots of toys,
Mother,
Memory.

Vertigo

> The woman wearing bifocal glasses
> glances down
> as she balances herself
> on her right foot
> by pressing her left palm
> against the wall
> of the elevator rising
> her right hand dropping
> to her left foot floating
> glances falling
> toward the shoe gliding
> fingers probing
> searching for the pebble hiding
> under the half-torn label
> of the shoe soaring that reads:
> "Do it more slowly next time."

Loving Mrs. Roosevelt

She wakes intricately
woven and punc-
tuated with gasps
from clasps
on her blouse intricately
woven and punc-
tuated with breasts
that inspire yet another charge
up San Juan Hill,
that speak softly
and carry a big heart
yes Teddy yes!

I Have Seen This

I have seen this -
The panic-stricken faces
On the terrified voices
Of fathers and mothers
Sisters sons and daughters
Brothers parents nannies
Husbands lovers and wives
New friends and old friends
On that moonless night
When the natives donned white hats
(The sailors wore white caps.)

I have seen this -
The rumble of the footsteps
Of brothers new friends
Nannies daughters mates
Husbands lovers sisters
Mothers fathers sons
Parents old friends wives
On the festive waves
Along the tilting deck
On that Night To Remember
When icebergs wore white caps
(The sailors wore white hats.)

I have seen all this -
Icebergs holding hands
Dancing the sailors' dance.
I have seen it twice:
The first time in black and white,
When Stanwyck was a doll
And I single, lithe...
Now in Technicolor,
With son daughter wife;
It's the nanny's night off.

Together

Come, let us now tremble together,
Together let us pass through the iron gate
Into the garden we planned together.

Come, let us walk now arm in arm, together,
Together let us stroll on our graveled path
Among the flowerbeds we planted together.

Come, here is the door we built together;
Together we carved and chiseled the oak
That we felled that spring we slept together.

Come, let us hold hands, our hands together,
Together let's climb these stairs of maple
Wearied by the steps of our years together.

Come, look about you; we stood here, together,
Together we wept on that summer's day
When I fled the stairs to be not together.

Come, let us enter this room together,
Together let's walk past the rosewood bed
Where you and I slept, sometimes together.

Come, open the window, let's stand together,
Together let's watch the twins near the roses
That on winter days we tamed together.

Look! don't you see the twins playing together?
Together they run, they jump, they giggle,
And when their hands touch, they blend together.

But wait. They have stopped...
They hold hands together....
Together they smile and turn away, these sisters,
Our future and our past...
They are leaving now...they fade...
Together.

Rossiniana

No, no, you are slow.
but then, don't you know
to read these lines well
 ?og tsum uoy tfel thgir

When skating on floe
 ,wobnair a gnisahc
left right slide your steps,
 .og uoy tfel tfel tfel

Right left we all row
wolgnoom eht hcaer ot
but right right right right
 .wolf snoom lla woh si

No no you're not slow,
 ,stom ni uoy nword I
but it's I who !setacoffus
 .throehtlahelpleh

Pleasures

Tell dear stranger, tell, where are pleasures born
That turn night to day, that lure the sorrow
From the hearts of men where no suns adorn
Into sunken graves beyond tomorrow?

Are they perhaps borne by a swallow's wing?
Or perhaps on peaks that invite the snow
To shed tears of joy heralding the spring,
To sate the thirst of the febrile fields? No...

These are joys of God, as also is man,
Imperceptible like unborn children.
But the joys of men, born of mind and pen,

They stroll arm in arm in meter and rhyme
Whistling chords and chime our hearts enliven
With dear pleasures shared, pleasures forgiven.